For What It's Worth ...
The Ministry of A Woman

*Fifty Years of Insights
From A Minister's Wife*

*by
Margaret Hicks*

Harrison House, Inc.
Tulsa, Oklahoma

Unless otherwise indicated, all Scripture quotations are taken from the *King James Version* of the Bible.

Scripture quotations marked AMP are taken from *The Amplified Bible, Old Testament*, copyright © 1964, 1987 by The Zondervan Publishing House, Grand Rapids, Michigan, or *The Amplified Bible, New Testament*, copyright © 1958, 1987 by The Lockman Foundation, La Habra, California.

Scripture quotations marked NKJV are taken from *The New King James Version* of the Bible, copyright © 1979, 1980, 1982, Thomas Nelson, Inc., Nashville, Tennessee.

The Scripture quotation from Rotherham is taken from *Rotherham's Emphasized Bible*, copyright © 1994 by Kregel Publishers, Grand Rapids, Michigan.

The Scripture quotation from J. B. Phillips is taken from *The New Testament in Modern English*, copyright © 1958, 1959, 1960, 1972, Macmillan Publishing Co., New York, New York.

Scripture quotations marked TCNT are taken from *The Twentieth Century New Testament*, Moody Bible Institute.

2nd Printing

For What It's Worth . . .
The Ministry of a Woman:
Fifty Years of Insights From A Minister's Wife
ISBN 0-89274-925-3
Copyright © 1995 by
Margaret Hicks
1034 La Sombra
San Marcos, CA 92069

Published by Harrison House, Inc.
P. O. Box 35035
Tulsa, OK 74153

Table of Contents

Foreword

Introduction

1	The Spirit of Excellence	13
2	Miriam	17
3	A Supportive Wife	23
4	Parental Love	29
5	The Fight of Faith for Marriage	35
6	No Place for Jealousy and Envy	39
7	A Sense of Humor	43
8	Women's Ministries	47
9	Huldah	51
10	Selflessness	55
11	The Little Member	59
12	Keeping Physically Fit	63
13	A Story of Submission	67
14	Dealing With Mistakes, Mischief, and Malice	71
15	Competition, by Dr. Roy Hicks	77

Reading furnishes the mind
only with materials of knowledge;
it is thinking that
makes what we read ours.[1]

John Locke

Foreword

When Margaret Hicks asked if I would write a foreword for this book, I felt very honored. Dick and I had only been married a few years when, as traveling evangelists, we conducted services at Roy and Margaret's church in Omaha, Nebraska. It was a heart-warming experience for me to see Margaret at close range. I was very impressed with her radiant joy, both in the home and in the church.

This book is a culmination of her many years in ministry, first as a pastor's wife and then as a supervisor's wife caring for several hundred churches. She now assists her husband in a very influential traveling ministry, transcending denominational lines.

Margaret's experiences speak to all kinds of women's ministries. Her words are rich in practical wisdom and are illustrated in a manner all women can relate to. For those starting out in ministry, Margaret's insights into scriptural solutions for common problems will offer great assistance. As a young evangelist's wife, I was very inexperienced and insecure in my role, and this book would have helped me tremendously at a time when I needed some guidelines.

You will appreciate her exhortation to keep a sense of humor at all costs. She deals wisely with such subjects as the good fight of faith, how to handle jealousy, and how to maintain a commitment to excellence.

For What It's Worth is priceless. I know you will enjoy reading this book as much as I have.

Betty Mills

Introduction

This book is in answer to the requests of some women in ministry, mostly younger, who were seeking answers to questions. It would not be possible to enumerate, nor would I presume to think I had the answer to every problem that exists. No two problems are alike, and no two people are alike! I have prayerfully endeavored to include a wide spectrum of subjects, and I am trusting the Holy Spirit to quicken to your spirit anything contained here that will be meaningful to you and may even open up a brand new chapter in your life!

My primary reason for writing this book is that I have a real desire to assist younger women. Never has there been a day like this day, with events moving so rapidly, so it is urgent that we "make the most" of what time we have.

Before going too far, let me make a statement concerning this book's contents. Much of it may seem to pertain to things that concern a pastor's wife, but the book is, in its entirety, written with the hope that there will be something for the pastor's wife, the deacon's wife, the bookkeeper's wife, the usher's wife, the parking lot attendant's wife — all women, married or unmarried. It is our prayer that it will add to your ongoing Christian experience and that it will bless and help you!

In Joel 2:28, it was prophesied that in the last days God would pour out His Spirit and that **your sons and your daughters shall prophesy**.... These certainly are "last days," and the opportunity for women to be active in ministry is *now*.

My husband made a study of the subject and found that 1 Timothy 2:12, rather than denying women the right to teach, gives them the privilege of teaching the Word of God as long as they do not usurp authority. This passage of Scripture should have been translated, "I will not suffer a

11

woman who is teaching to usurp authority over a man." This is in support of G. Campbell Morgan, in a book now out of print, who acknowledged the right of women to teach God's Word.

In this day we are more challenged than ever before to be godly women who are *strong, but not overbearing; wise, but not arrogant; courageous, but not insolent; confident, but not defiant.* There is a climate in the world in these last days that aids and abets a spirit of angry antagonism. The woman of God must guard her heart against it. It is insidious and can entangle you before you are aware it is happening!

No personal agenda is worth jeopardizing our relationship with our Lord Jesus. We are on a journey, and our destination is Heaven. We must be prepared to recognize the tools Satan uses in his evil schemes to destroy anything and everything that is good and godly.

We have endeavored to write about subjects that, having observed through the years, are for the most part areas where ministries have been "made" or "broken." These are "stumbling stones" that can be turned into "stepping stones" if some effort is applied!

Margaret Hicks

1

The Spirit of Excellence

Someone has said that "good" is the enemy of "best." If we do not want the best, then we are committed to settling for that which is merely good. However, I believe God wants us to do more than just "get along" in our place of ministry.

The best illustration of what I am trying to say comes from a good friend of ours. When he became a father for the first time, he looked down at that tiny little baby and said, "You've never been a baby before, and I've never been a father before." For a moment, he panicked at the thought of the responsibility. Then he looked to God and prayed, asking for a "spirit of excellence and the spirit of relax!" He prayed for "excellence" because he wanted to do his best, and "relax" because all of his efforts as a father from then on were to be *with the help of God*!

We can have both excellence and peace. The spirit of excellence should not be worn as a badge of a militant, overstressed conqueror who is victorious through personal triumph. It is a combination of what you determine to accomplish coupled with the knowledge that **it is God who works in you both to will and to do for His good pleasure** (Phil. 2:13 NKJV).

Good is not bad, but it falls far short of what is possible. *Good* is performing the letter of the Word apart from the supernatural guidance and empowering of the Holy Spirit. *Best* is seeing in your spirit the vast potential you possess by fearlessly claiming God's promises and walking in them by His Spirit. "Oh," but you say, "this is the pastor's domain, not mine." Not so! I am *not* talking about a strong-minded, managerial woman.

Adam Clarke's *Commentary* shares a little rhyme about this type of woman:

> *Ill thrives the hapless family that shows*
>
> *A cock that's silent and a hen that crows.*
>
> *I know not which lives most unnatural lives,*
>
> *Obeying husbands or commanding wives!*[2]

This is not the picture I am painting here! I am talking about a strong, confident, Word-oriented woman who will be able to stand alongside her minister husband and strengthen him with her support.

There is a fine line between *good* and *best*, but with commitment and prayer, the line is identified. There is no guide that can be established as the standard we should all follow to find this place of excellence in the peace of God. Each believer must seek this place for themselves, finding God's will for their lives and doing it.

With Billy Graham's wife, Ruth, it was a life of devotion to the home and raising their five children while Billy obeyed God's call on his life. With countless numbers of women, it will be determining a life of excellence in a vastly different setting.

In your marriage, it could be that your husband wants you to take a very active part in his ministry, or it could be just the opposite, that he desires your sphere of activity to be in the home. Or again, you may share in each responsibility.

God does not reward according to the grandness of our ministries, our immense congregations, or the vastness of our influence. He rewards for one virtue alone — *faithfulness*. Therefore, we must keep our eyes on the goal.

That goal is "faithful excellence" in doing God's will in whatever field He has placed us.

The pastor's wife who has stood alongside her husband faithfully and encouraged him as he pastors the flock God has given him, regardless of size, along with every woman who is faithful in following God's will for her life, will hear the same words that great Christian soulwinners throughout Church history will hear: **Well done, thou good and faithful servant...enter thou into the joy of the Lord** (Matt. 25:21).

This is not to say we should ever be satisfied with small congregations. In light of the multitudes of unsaved people who surround us, we need to be praying and witnessing unceasingly, believing for increase!

Regardless of where God has placed us as women, our greatest concern is to do our utmost to serve Him well. In Philippians 3:8, the Apostle Paul said, **I count all things but loss for the excellency of the knowledge of Christ Jesus my Lord.** Paul counted things that were of personal gain to him as loss.

How important is it to always strive for the spirit of excellence? If a leader, endeavoring to teach others, has a failure in his or her own life, all of the teaching is undermined by the instability of the leader. As a result, many lives could be affected adversely. As a teacher, you cannot teach effectively if your life does not reflect the lesson.

For Henrietta Mears, a well-known Christian educator of another generation, *faithful excellence* was: "There is no magic in small plans. When I consider my ministry, I think of the world. Anything less than that would not be worthy of the Lord or His plan for my life."[3]

The Corinthians were referred to as epistles, **known and read of all men** (2 Cor. 3:2). This is why we must strive for excellence, because not only are we an example to those we teach, but the world is watching!

2
Miriam

The Bible is a remarkable mirror. In a familiar children's story, the wicked witch says, "Mirror, mirror on the wall, who's the fairest of them all?" If the mirror had answered truthfully, it would have said, "You're ugly!" But it was different than the mirrors we have on our walls. Ours only reveal to us what others can see — the external covering of our inner man.

The inner man is what the Bible mirrors. It tells the truth, and no manner of denial makes it any different. Just as a vanity mirror shows defects in our physical countenance, *the mirror of God's Word reflects our spiritual defects.* Unlike *the mirror on the wall, however, it can also show us the cure!*

The wisdom to work contentedly, without striving for promotion within our sphere of influence, is just as important as the God-given talents and abilities we possess. God's textbook, the Bible, is our book of instruction about how and in what manner these talents and abilities are to be used. There will never be a problem of misuse if we commit these abilities to God and then let the Bible instruct us, through the Holy Spirit, how to use them.

In the book of Exodus, there is the remarkable story of the deliverance of God's people from the tyranny in Egypt. Joseph, who had great favor with Pharaoh, had died, and there arose a new ruler in Egypt who "knew not Joseph." Because of his fear of the Jews, there came a time of great persecution and affliction, finally resulting in the king's

17

decree that all male Israelite children should be killed at birth.

It was at this time that an Israelite baby, later to be known as Moses, was born. His mother, knowing he would be killed if he was discovered, made a small boat of rushes, placed three-month-old Moses in it, and put it in the river.

Moses' sister, Miriam, a little girl at the time, watched. When she saw the daughter of Pharaoh come down to the river to bathe, she quickly thought of a plan. She knew Moses would be discovered and something would have to be done to protect him. Her leadership ability and quick wit were evident very early in life.

When Pharaoh's daughter discovered the little boat with Moses in it, he was crying, and even though she knew it was a Hebrew child, her heart was touched with compassion. Miriam observed all of this, and she recognized that Pharaoh's daughter felt pity for her little brother. She boldly stepped forth and offered to find a Hebrew nurse to care for the baby. Permission was given, so immediately she brought her mother. Not only did Moses have his own mother to raise him, she was paid for the privilege of doing so!

This scenario shows Miriam to be ingenious and quick-witted far beyond her years. As her story unfolds, we will see that those who have been endowed with unusual intelligence will have to give account for how they use it. Luke 12:48b says, **For unto whomsoever much is given, of him shall be much required: and to whom men have committed much, of him they will ask the more.**

Moses grew up in the household of Pharaoh, but upon slaying an Egyptian guard to protect a Jew, he fled to the wilderness for forty years. Eventually God led him back to Egypt and Pharaoh's court, where his mission was to free Israel from Pharaoh's tyranny. Chapters 2 through 12 of Exodus record the history of Moses' life up to Passover, the slaying of the firstborn in every household in Egypt that did not have the blood of the lamb on their doorposts. It was this event which finally caused Pharaoh to let the Israelites go, and now begins the story with which this chapter is concerned.

We hear of Miriam again in Exodus 15, after the miraculous crossing of the Red Sea. Moses and the children of Israel sang a triumphal song, glorifying God and exalting His great name. Miriam, acknowledged as a prophetess, took up a timbrel and continued to lead the women in praise with singing and dancing. She was held in high esteem and continued in this position of honor for some time. She is mentioned as equal with both Moses and Aaron in Micah 6:4.

Miriam, though she did not know it, was in a place of great danger. She was elevated to a place of honor and public display, a leader to whom people were to pay respect and give heed to her words. If there was ever a time in her life when she needed spiritual insight, it was then! Counted as one who could lead the people into the very presence of God in praise and worship, she was vulnerable to attack.

Satan always targets God's servants who, if he can cause them to fall, will discourage the greatest number of believers. You are in your most precarious position in a time of success and achievement. Previously, your beliefs never carried much weight, but now everyone seeks your opinion.

Have you noticed that most of the trouble we have among Christians is caused by faultfinding and being vocal about it? This was Miriam's problem. She criticized Moses for marrying an Ethiopian woman! It was none of her business, but obviously she felt the headiness of her position. After all, wasn't it Miriam who was instrumental in saving Moses when he was a baby? Wasn't she older than either Moses or Aaron? Was not her voice equally as important?

It is true that many Old Testament saints did not have the Word as a mirror to correct and instruct them, but God dealt with them in a tangible way that we are not exposed to very often in the New Covenant. In the middle of this time of criticizing and discontent the Bible says, **And the Lord heard it** (Num. 12:2). You can be assured, He always hears our murmuring!

God's action was swift. He requested all three — Moses, Aaron, and Miriam — to come to the tabernacle of the congregation. The Lord came down in the pillar of cloud. (v. 5.) They felt His anger as He set things in order, leaving no doubt that Moses was the prophet among them, the one to whom He would speak **face to face** (v. 8 NKJV).

To my knowledge, no one has been smitten with leprosy because of criticism and faultfinding lately. But when Christians become involved in backbiting, it is wrong. The Word, their conscience, and common sense indicate that it is wrong, and there is a price to pay for it.

Galatians 6:7,8a says:

> **Be not deceived; God is not mocked: for whatsoever a man soweth, that shall he also reap.**
>
> **For he that soweth to his flesh shall of the flesh reap corruption.**

As the glory of the Lord departed, Aaron looked upon Miriam, who had become leprous. Moses sought the Lord to heal her, but to no avail. She was shut out of the camp for seven days, after which time her leprosy was healed. (See Num. 12.)

Seven days was a long enough time for Miriam to consider how wrong she was to be lifted up in pride and meddle in affairs that were none of her business! It is truly amazing how swiftly the enemy can move in, as a master deceiver, right at the pinnacle of our spiritual experience. He knows our weaknesses.

The next mention of Miriam is in Numbers 20:1: **Miriam died there, and was buried there.** From a child, she was especially used of the Lord. She could have been remembered in history in the same way as the woman who anointed Jesus with precious ointment is remembered. In Mark 14:9, as Jesus prepared for Calvary, He said, **Wheresoever this gospel shall be preached throughout the whole world, this also that she hath done shall be spoken of for a memorial of her.** How sad that this very special lady, Miriam, should be memorialized forever in the context of the judgment of the Lord God on her, and then died in obscurity. (Deut. 24:9.)

What is the greatest lesson we can learn from Miriam? It is true that in these last days God is pouring out His Spirit on all flesh, and He has said His sons and daughters shall prophesy. As godly women, we are privileged to teach and preach His Word.

Our greatest concern should be to find our place of service, great or small, and give every ounce of our spiritual energy to the fulfilling of it. When a measure of success comes, remember Miriam! She had it all, yet lost out on God's best because she reached beyond where God had placed her.

3
A Supportive Wife

In her book *Creative Counterpart*, Linda Dillow relates an incident about a business opportunity where three important positions needed to be filled. A committee interviewed many applicants, and the names of twenty men were chosen. However, instead of interviewing the twenty men, they interviewed their wives! They came up with nine winners.[4]

What element was it in the nine women, who were not necessarily beautiful, super-intelligent, or poised, that made the interviewers choose their husbands? They possessed one important ingredient — *they were supportive of their husbands.*

What does it mean to be supportive? *Webster's Dictionary* says it means "to be an advocate, a champion, a comforter in time of need." If you desire to be an effective minister's wife, this will certainly do for a starter!

Full-time ministers always feel the weight of their call, especially young ministers who are on the threshold of ministry. But whether you are just now beginning as ministers or have been involved in the Lord's work for many years, the commitment to give one's very best never lessens. And the unfailing strength of a wife who is supportive of her husband makes a great contribution to a flourishing ministry!

I recall talking with the wife of a young minister who had just taken his first pastoral appointment. She confided in me about how nervous and apprehensive she was about her husband's ability to preach. She confessed that her stomach tied up in knots when he stepped into the pulpit.

I tried to encourage her that it would get better with time and experience, but she was never able to overcome her fearfulness. Eventually, she conveyed her lack of confidence to her husband, and though he had great potential, it was never realized. She failed to give him the encouragement and support he needed in those crucial years.

Do we really understand the power of the words we speak every day? As a child I remember hearing, "Sticks and stones may break my bones, but words will never hurt me!" But they do! Proverbs 18:8 tells us, **The words of a talebearer are as wounds, and they go down into the innermost parts of the belly.** That is as deep as a wound can get, and it can have lasting consequences. Many of the insecurities we fight as adults started when, as children, someone embarrassed us or said angry, hurtful things that lodged in our memories.

I remember walking on the beach along the Oregon coast with two of my best friends one summer. Somehow we found ourselves talking about the subject of insecurity. I commented that, as a child, I was very self-conscious because of a genetic irregularity on my mother's side of our family that kept the nail of the index finger and the thumb from developing normally.

Both friends said in unison, "I never noticed that before!" Then one of my friends spoke up and said, "You know, it's true. I have always had a feeling of insecurity because I am not very tall but my feet are long." I looked down. I had never noticed before, but actually her feet were large for her petite size!

My other friend then said, "I'll confess I have always been self-conscious because my legs are bowed." I looked down and, sure enough, they were somewhat bowed! She said, "When I was a little girl, we visited friends on a farm. We were all trying to catch a small pig. I almost had my hands on it, and it turned and ran right between my legs!"

Too often we let things that no one else even notices become real issues when we should be ignoring them! When we were children, we lacked the maturity to handle our emotions. Now, we let fear, insecurity, lack of confidence, self-consciousness, and all of the other negative feelings the enemy uses against us to become so big, they consume much of our attention.

We forget that God made us to be overcomers! Rather than calling attention to the negatives, enumerate every positive ability and characteristic that you see in your husband. Maybe you have accentuated the negatives so long that you have become blind to all of his good qualities! If you are single, but you acknowledge having a problem of nit-picking or criticizing, believe the scripture that says, **Death and life are in the power of the tongue** (Prov. 18:21). We can kill or give life by the things we say!

In the New Covenant, James 3:2 AMP says, **For we all often stumble and fall and offend in many things. And if anyone does not offend in speech [never says the wrong things], he is a fully developed character and a perfect man, able to control his whole body and to curb his entire nature.**

How can we best understand the word *supportive*? Perhaps by looking at the word that means just the opposite. The word *adversary* means "a competitor, opponent, rival, or antagonist." "Impossible!" you say. "No minister's wife I know personally resembles such a person!" And I agree. I have never met such a person — where she and her husband are successful in ministry.

We are not talking about an on-going adversarial lifestyle. We seldom see that. The very fact that you are involved in ministry is evidence that you want to do well and succeed. It is not overt, intended, and repeated negative behavior that we are talking about.

The Song of Solomon, chapter 2, verse 15, speaks of **the little foxes, that spoil the vines.** These were not predatory animals that plundered entire fields, but small animals that would leap and nip at the clusters of grapes hanging down within their reach. The entire crop wasn't endangered, but there was enough damage that the quality and quantity of the product was affected.

A ministry might not be completely destroyed by competition, rivalry, or antagonism in the home, but it will be hindered and kept from its full potential. This principle applies to the unmarried as well as to the married. Negative, contradictory conduct will cause confusion. James 3:16 says, **For where envying and strife is, there is confusion and every evil work.**

First Peter 5:8 tells us, **Be sober, be vigilant.** *The Amplified Version* of this verse reads, **Be well balanced (temperate, sober of mind), be vigilant and cautious at all times, for that enemy of yours, the devil, roams around like a lion roaring [in fierce hunger], seeking someone to seize upon and devour.**

When we give in to pettiness, littleness, and peevishness, we stop being supportive and fail to resist Satan. Then we are in danger of standing in the role of an *adversary* instead of a *supportive helper.*

Ephesians 5:22 instructs us, as wives, to **submit [ourselves] unto [our] own husbands, as unto the Lord.** In this same context, it describes the love that a Christian husband is to have for his wife. How could you not love and submit to your husband when he loves you **as Christ also loved the church?** (v. 25) This is a picture of a loving husband who is concerned first about the well-being and happiness of his wife. Verse 28 says he is to love her as he loves his own body, and it speaks of nourishing and cherishing her. Finally, he is to love her as he loves himself. (v. 33).

Each person has her own arena of obedience, submission and adapting. There is a wonderful reward for a peaceful, loving home. Strong ministry emanates from such an atmosphere. It will serve as an illustrated sermon to those to whom you minister!

Most of us desire to be "an advocate, a champion, a comforter in time of need," but because we are so human, we are not always what we want to be in this area! Nevertheless, we should make it a goal and press toward it. As one wise pastor's wife said, *"I back him up when he is right, and help him back up when he is wrong."*

4
Parental Love

Let's talk about children. Titus 2:3,4 says:

> The aged women likewise, that they be in behaviour as becometh holiness, not false accusers, not given to much wine, teachers of good things;
>
> That they may teach the young women to be sober, to love their husbands, *to love their children.*

The many years I have lived designates me to be one who is to be a **teacher of good things.** There is nothing closer to our hearts than the desire to see children raised in an atmosphere of love, being taught about God and His love.

There are a number of subjects to consider in these verses, but because of the nature of this chapter, we will consider the last four words, *to love their children.* It is hard to imagine that anyone would have to be reminded to love their children! Yet, in the news every day we hear appalling accounts of children who are aborted, abandoned, treated cruelly, and abused.

What does *love* mean? *Webster's Dictionary* describes it as "deep devotion or intense fondness." In Titus, where *love* is used in relation to children it means "to cherish, to hold dear, and nourish."

The 13th chapter of 1 Corinthians, AMP, tells me that if I do not have God's love in me, **I am nothing — a useless nobody.** Love is the greatest of the three grand words used in this chapter: faith, hope, and love. It is the only one of the

29

three that we will need throughout eternity! Faith and hope will have fulfilled their mission, but love, in its many facets, is the greatest — both now and then.

There are scores of books, both Christian and secular, written on the subject of raising children. Raising them successfully continues to be one of the greatest challenges we face. There is no pattern or set of rules that every parent could adopt as the plan by which to raise their children. There are far too many variables, differences, and personalities involved. But there are some basic principles to which we can all give heed.

First, there is *real* versus *unreal* love. No Christian parent wants to be in danger of showing "bogus" or "pretended" love toward their children. If we say *words of love* and continually show *actions of impatience and anger*, then we belie our words! It is difficult to teach a child to love if all he ever hears is disagreement and anger. The *best gift* we can ever give our children is an atmosphere of love in the home.

This is not to say we won't have disagreements occasionally. Someone once asked an internationally known evangelist's wife if she and her husband always agreed. Her answer was, "No, if we always agreed, one of us would be unnecessary!" However, it is possible to disagree without displaying anger and resentment.

Second, I encourage Christian parents to dedicate their children to the Lord at an early age. This is a practice that is confirmed in the Bible. It is an act that will give you strength and confidence during the years of training and discipline (always with love, even if it is tough love) that will follow. This sets the direction of their lives and indicates to the Lord that you are giving your children to Him, that you want Him to have preeminence in their lives. It says to the Lord that you believe His Word, **Train up a child in the way he should go: and [even] when he is old, he will not depart from it** (Prov. 22:6).

Two sons and a daughter were born to us, and we love them dearly. Our firstborn son is now in Heaven. We miss him greatly, but it is where we all look forward to being soon with great anticipation!

When our children were growing up, we can remember times when God was not in all of their thoughts! Now that they have matured, they truly love God and live for Him. I believe an important factor took place when we dedicated them to the Lord as infants. By faith, we set the direction of their lives by that simple, sincere act.

Third, as Christian parents, we must seek God daily for wisdom in every decision that surfaces as a result of simply being a parent! Someone has said, "Life is the only experience that gives you the test first and the lesson second!" One great fact is evident though, and that is, we must be consistent with our children in giving them equal amounts of *love* and *discipline*! Either one, used exclusively, will produce maladjusted or spoiled lives.

Believe it or not, there are some hazards of being in ministry and raising children. One incident comes to mind. When our two sons were teenagers, they had several friends in the church — all normal, lively, happy young people.

I was in the church office one day when one of the deacons came up to me and said, with an air of exasperation, "I don't know what we are going to do with the young people in this church, and your two boys are the worst!"

This was a ripe opportunity to explode, or use a little wisdom and turn a potentially distressing situation around. I simply smiled, patted him on the arm and said, "Brother, we'll just keep praying for them, and they will be all right!"

You say, "How could you stay so calm and not be angry when your children were being attacked?" Proverbs 4:7

31

advises, **With all thy getting get understanding.** I understood something. This man was in his sixties, and he and his wife had a son later in life, who was now a teenager. Their son was no worse than any other active, spirited boy, but because the father was older, it was hard for him to cope with all of the vitality and energy of a teenager. He was not really angry with our boys, but he had to vent his frustration and fears, and I was the one to receive it.

Fourth, remember that children whose parents are in the ministry are blessed of God! I remember hearing a pastor's son complain that he had such a hard life because he had to change schools so much. When I heard that I thought, "Pastors' children are not the only ones who have to transfer from school to school occasionally." Parents have many vocations that cause them to be transferred, sometimes even out of the country and into strange, exotic situations.

Our oldest son, Roy, Jr., remembered being reluctant about moving when he and his brother, Jim, were small. After he grew up, in retrospect, he confessed that all of the experiences of living in different cities, and the two years we traveled in a motor home in missionary conference work, enabled him (really, all three of our children) to visit sites in the East that were rich in our country's history. This exposure was a great advantage and blessing.

You can encourage your children that if you are facing a move, it is something they will appreciate later on, even if they don't now. It will add to their memories and experiences, and their lives will be all the richer for it.

Finally, perhaps the greatest thing we can do for our children as parents is to *love one another!* Nothing will contribute more to a child's well-being and adjustment than growing up in a home where love and appreciation between the parents are evident. It is comparatively rare to find maladjusted, angry young people from a peaceful, loving home environment.

Most of the young people who end up in juvenile hall come from homes where they are abused and hurt physically and emotionally. One of the greatest ministries we can become involved in is the ministry to young people who are growing up without an understanding of God's love.

Keep this ministry in perspective, however! We must love and reach out to troubled young people in every way we can, but the children we are *totally* responsible for are the children God places in our homes. We must give an account for them. Therefore, we must be especially diligent to love, instruct, and discipline our own first.

Behold, children are a heritage of the Lord, the fruit of the womb is a reward.

Like arrows in the hand of a warrior, so are the children of one's youth.

Psalm 127:3,4 NKJV

5
The Fight of Faith for Marriage

As a pastor's wife or a woman in ministry, you will have many opportunities to answer questions and minister to women who will come to you when their marriages are in trouble. In this role, the Holy Spirit will always be your greatest source of help. Great caution must be used when you give advice to another. Only God can help us to know what is helpful and what is harmful.

The phrase, "fighting for a marriage," brings to mind a picture of hostility, although that is not what is intended in this writing. The "fighting" is not to be husband against wife or wife against husband — *but both against the enemy* — united in a common cause to defeat Satan in his evil intent to kill love, steal peace, and destroy the home.

An enemy so dedicated to destruction can only be stopped by a superior force — the greater force of God's Word — which is **quick** [swift], **and powerful** [vigorous], **and sharper** [more acute] **than any two-edged sword** (Heb. 4:12).

In the Old Testament, under the law people were motivated by the Ten Commandments. In the New Testament, believers should be motivated by the law of love. **For in Jesus Christ neither circumcision availeth any thing, nor uncircumcision; but faith which worketh by love** (Gal. 5:6).

The fight of faith is an ongoing fight, comprised of many skirmishes. The fight of faith of a Christian woman married to a Christian man will differ from that of a Christian woman married to an unbeliever.

In the epistles, the Apostle Paul says, **But if the unbelieving depart, let him depart. A brother or a sister is not under bondage in such cases: but God has called us to peace** (1 Cor. 7:15).

To the Christian woman who is married to an unbeliever who chooses to live with her, however, the Bible instructs, **Likewise, ye wives, be in subjection to your own husbands; that, if any obey not the word, they also may without the word be won by the conversation [lifestyle] of the wives** (1 Pet. 3:1).

This means the Holy Spirit may not use her words, but He will use her "living out" the Word, just as He would use the written Word of God to bring conviction for sin. This verse suggests that the Holy Spirit could be hindered in His work of conviction of sin if there is an overuse of argument and "preaching." The wife will have many opportunities to *demonstrate* her faith, motivated by love!

Scripture gives us a beautiful balance in how to interpret it. Peter tells us that a husband may be won to the Lord by a wife's godly life. Paul tells us that she is to continue her godly living with her mate as long as **he be pleased to dwell with her** (1 Cor. 7:13). (If he continually beats and brutalizes her, it is evident that he is not pleased to dwell with her, and she is no longer bound to stay with him.)

Living a godly life before an unsaved husband is where your will, consecration, and dedication come in. One of the greatest examples of a wife who was determined to win her husband to Jesus occurred in a church we pastored in Ohio. We will call her Jane, although that is not her real name. She was a staunch member and worker in the church, but her husband wanted nothing to do with her "religion" and repeatedly told her so. Still, he "was pleased to dwell with her" and did not mistreat her.

My husband visited them occasionally, as good pastors did in those days, and Jane's husband would make a statement of his attitude by blowing cigar smoke in my husband's face! Jane never became discouraged, but kept praying in faith, knowing in her heart that he would come to the Lord.

Finally, he agreed to attend a service with her. When the altar call was given, the Spirit of God convicted him of sin, and he accepted Jesus as his Savior. Someone who noticed that Jane was just standing nearby and watching said to her, "You should be the happiest person in this room. You've prayed for your husband for years, and tonight he is finally getting saved!"

Jane said, "You don't understand, I rejoiced over this a long time ago." She knew something that is important for women to know who are praying for an unsaved husband. The first time she prayed for her husband, she saw him, through the eyes of faith, *saved and walking with Jesus*. She began *then* to rejoice over his salvation.

Jane never deviated from that position of faith, and she never "preached" to him about being saved. She truly demonstrated the scripture, **Now faith is the substance of things hoped for, the evidence of things not seen** (Heb. 11:1).

Unfortunately, not all marriages do as well as Jane's and many are divorced. In all of our years of ministry, I cannot think of any question that has been more shrouded with confusion than the subject of divorce when it involves believers.

Much confusion has resulted among Christians because of disagreement concerning the interpretation of scriptures in the New Testament. In the gospels, divorce is treated the same as it is in the Old Testament. When questioned by the Pharisees (who were trying to tempt Him) Jesus taught that no divorce was justified except for fornication. (See Matt. 19:1-9.)

Divorce in a Christian union should never be a consideration, but in extreme conditions, such as where one spouse is continually unfaithful or is violent and abusive, it can happen. As long as a man and a woman can stay together without harming each other, however, there is hope for reconciliation. Divorce does not solve problems; it causes other problems.

A friend shared his sorrow with us over the divorce of his parents. Neither parent would ever capitulate and say they were sorry when they argued. What had once been a loving marriage was torn apart because of their stubborn, unyielding attitudes. There was a divorce, and in time his mother married again. One of the tragedies of this broken home was that, though the wife remarried, she still loved her first husband. They will never have the opportunity to erase the past with forgiveness and start again.

This chapter began with words of caution concerning how we advise those who come to us for help. Many churches now, because of unfortunate experiences and lawsuits, have counselors on staff who are trained, experienced, and have an understanding of all the ramifications of counseling troubled people. If you are approached by a woman in a troubled marriage, encourage her to see one of these trained counselors.

God's design for our lives is a perfect one, and the closer we can pattern our lives after His design, the happier we will be. As we conform our individual lives and our marriages to His Word, we will most certainly win the fight of faith for our marriages!

6
No Place for Jealousy and Envy

The subject of jealousy, as taught in the Bible, has many facets. First, there is the jealousy that God has for His people, which is infinitely different than man's jealousy. God spoke through the Apostle Paul in 2 Corinthians 11:2, **For I am jealous over you with godly jealousy: for I have espoused you to one husband, that I may present you as a chaste virgin to Christ.** The jealousy that God has for the Church is solicitous, protective, and vigilant.

Then there is the jealousy of man as revealed throughout history in envy, resentment, and suspicion. In this chapter, we will deal with man's jealousy, a subject that is as old as time. It started with the first two children ever born, Cain and Abel, and resulted in the first murder. Men and women called to the ministry of the Word have had their lives ruined by the effects of this tool of Satan.

Public figures will always be the subject of someone's admiration. We have to accept that as fact. In ministry, the larger the congregation or following grows, the greater the number of admirers. A woman married to a man involved in any public ministry must learn to handle that fact with equanimity and trust and remember that people see him always and only in the best of circumstances.

In many congregations, there are young, pretty women; capable, competent women; talented, gifted women; *and* women who may admire another woman's husband. In Matthew 13 we find the parable of the wheat and the tares. A man sowed good seed in his field, but while he slept the enemy came and sowed tares. When the seed grew, tares appeared right along with the wheat. This is a picture of the Church. Not every dilemma caused by jealousy in the congregation is generated by Satan. The tares are there right along with the wheat, and sometimes it is just as much the weakness of the person involved as it is the influence of Satan.

Proverbs 30:32b says, **If thou hast thought evil, lay thine hand upon thy mouth.** Good advice! Most of the arguments and fighting caused by jealousy could have been avoided if fuel (angry words) had not been added. If you react in an unpleasant, disagreeable way, you will exacerbate the very problem you want to go away.

There are two things to be considered: 1) It could be your imagination. If you become angered over something that is only what you imagine, it could and probably will cause deep wounding, not just with the other woman, but with your husband; and 2) If someone really lacks wisdom in her display of interest in your husband, it will not be your jealousy toward her but your display of trust in your husband that will be a source of strength to him and bring healing to the situation.

It is not God's will that there ever be anger and jealousy among Christians, but the enemy who goes about **as a roaring lion** (1 Pet. 5:8) is ever aware of opportunities to **kill, steal, and destroy** (John 10:10) by the use of this tool.

After the service one Sunday morning in a church we pastored, someone came to me and related that the wife of one of our members accused another woman of working in a particular church just so she could be near her husband — a potential catastrophe! If we could deal with just the two people involved, it could be easily solved. But people always take sides and everybody gets involved!

When my husband and I got home, I told him what I had heard. Standing in the middle of the living room, we took hands and bound the enemy according to Matthew 16:19, gave God thanks, and then had dinner! By the time of the evening service, the two women had gotten together, apologies were made and accepted, and the enemy lost another battle! *Application of scriptural principles with faith will always result in victory!*

Most of our problems with jealousy come as a result of something that is spoken which isn't necessarily accurate or true. Either we say it or someone else says it, and in no time it is magnified out of proportion and can result in calamity. The Bible, especially the book of Proverbs, has much to say concerning the tongue. A good exercise is to go through Proverbs and underline every verse that has to do with the tongue and the words we speak.

Actually, there are two areas over which we can become jealous, natural things and spiritual things. Natural things include everything from talents and personality to physical appearance. Do you sometimes look at others a little enviously and say, "I'm not as pretty as she is," "I can't play the piano," "I am embarrassed to get up in front of people," or "I'm so awkward I can't do anything right"?

First, I recommend my husband's book, *Healing Your Insecurities*, published by Harrison House. His treatment of the subject has brought healing to multitudes of men and women. And second, stop letting the enemy rob you of precious years of service to the Lord. When you make statements or entertain thoughts that undercut or minimize your value to the Lord, you play right into the enemy's hands.

Accept your looks and make the very best of what you have. Everyone has a unique beauty. And don't condemn yourself if you are not a piano virtuoso, a prima donna, or a sought-after public speaker. Very few are! Instead, take the talents you have and let God multiply them. He can do miracles, just as He did with the widow's oil in 1 Kings 17 and the little boy's lunch in Matthew 14.

On the other hand, there will be spiritually gifted people through whom God works with "a word" that will directly minister to a situation. These people, very often women, are blessed with an unusual sensitivity to the spirit world, and God can use them in a very special way to warn, instruct, and caution a minister.

Guard your feelings. Do not give any place to envy or resentment because someone has counseled or warned your husband through the Holy Spirit's urging. Rather, thank God for this wonderful gift. It does not minimize you as his helpmeet. Instead, it gives him a great feeling of confidence knowing his wife is not given to unjustified resentment.

Romans 12:5,6 says we are one body, having gifts that differ according to the grace given to us. None of us would want to hamper or obstruct the Body of Christ in its work in the world. The world is too needy. (Read Romans 12:4-8.)

Rather than envying another's spiritual gifts or natural endowments and abilities, seek the Holy Spirit and read the Word of God for help, guidance, and comfort. Spend time in the Lord's presence, and He will reveal your uniqueness to you.

The real reward of a life dedicated to serving Jesus without jealousy and envy is described in Proverbs 31:30,31:

> **Favour is deceitful, and beauty is vain: but a woman that feareth the Lord, she shall be praised.**
>
> **Give her the fruit of her hands; and let her own works praise her in the gates.**

7

A Sense of Humor

Does humor have a place in the ministry? Indeed! It may be one of your best tools for surviving some of the trials that come as a result of being in ministry. In his book, *He Who Laughs...Lasts and Lasts*, my husband writes, "Laughter is joy flowing." How apt!

A warm sense of humor can turn an embarrassing, discouraging, or tense situation into a laughable one. Come on now, haven't we all learned that we laugh about those incidents later? Then why not learn to laugh now and spare yourself the agony of embarrassment?

My husband and I have learned that laughter is not a mere emotion, but an attitude of living! Periodically (but I am working on it) I fail to record checks properly when I write them. We have come to the place where we laugh about it. After all, when the check comes back we'll find out where it went!

On the other hand, we also laugh when I ask my husband, "How in the world can you spray toothpaste clear to the top of the bathroom mirror when you brush your teeth?" Abundant opportunities like these avail themselves every day of our lives, making us so glad that we have learned the importance of this precious attitude of living!

Smith Wigglesworth, a well-known English evangelist who went on to be with the Lord in 1947, told of the period of his life when he was a backslider. He had a great argument with his wife, and he locked her out of the house!

She went on to church and when she got home, the doors were still locked, so she slept on the steps by the back door. When he unlocked the doors in the morning, she let herself in and busily went about fixing breakfast as though nothing had happened. Ignoring Smith's earlier temper tantrum, she asked him what he wanted to eat. They looked at each other and burst out laughing. What a woman of great wisdom! Her practical, Christian treatment of this situation brought peace where there could have been permanent damage to a relationship.

The Bible has much to say about joy, laughter and happiness. Proverbs 15:13 says, **A merry heart maketh a cheerful countenance.** Instead of putting so much confidence in all of the trumpeted beauty oils and creams, why not try laughing a lot? All of the beauty aids in the world will not stop the onslaughts of time and its effect upon our appearance.

Those tiny little "crow's feet" lines will begin to show eventually. You cannot keep that from happening, but you can determine what kind of lines they will be — laugh lines or frown lines! The final word is, "We end up with the face we deserve," so why not begin today to learn to laugh? Let this wonderful attitude of living become a part of your life!

Proverbs 17:22a AMP says, **A happy heart is good medicine and a cheerful mind works healing.** A recently published report enumerated a number of positive effects on one's health that result from laughter. One of them was that when laughter is present, the body pumps adrenaline — a good remedy for fatigue and listlessness!

Another effect was that the brain releases endorphins (pain killers) when we laugh. Sounds like a better answer than the over-the-counter medicines we fill our cupboards with! I am not saying to quit taking what your doctor has prescribed, but give God's Word a chance to prove itself in your life by learning to laugh. With perseverance you will come to have a merry heart — and enjoy the fruit of it!

Have you ever said, "I laughed 'til I cried?" This is another wonderful physical benefit of laughter. Your eyes are cleansed! Smog, dust, and chemicals are washed away.

And how about all of those times when you are uptight and tense? Sometimes we don't even know why we are stressed, but a good dose of laughter is a great muscle relaxer. It won't do away with the incident or problem that brought on the taut nerves, but it will allow you to tackle it in a far more effective frame of mind.

Psalm 63:5b,6 says:

> **...And my mouth shall praise thee with joyful lips:**
> [the *Rotherham Translation* says, "With joyfully shouting lips"]:
> **When I remember thee upon my bed, and meditate on thee in the night watches.**

However, "If you plan to shout joyfully in the middle of the night, you had better warn your husband first!"

Second Corinthians 6:10 covers the depth, length, and breadth of the emotions we experience. **As sorrowful, yet alway rejoicing; as poor, yet making many rich; as having nothing, and yet possessing all things.** If we can say this, then we have begun to learn what it is to live in the Spirit.

Our goal should be to have our spirit so indwelt by the Holy Spirit that we are no longer living in the soulish realm that is servant to the experiences that come as a result of living in the devil's world. The J. B. Phillips translation says it this way: *We know sorrow, yet our joy is inextinguishable.* Say this out loud!

This is not a call to suddenly become a "funny woman," but to begin to turn difficult, depressing, and discouraging circumstances into stepping stones by learning to laugh about them.

I recall hearing Dr. Kenneth E. Hagin tell of an experience that happened many years ago when he was pastoring. His wife, Oretha, came home and said, "Guess what I just heard?" He asked what it was and she said, "Someone saw you in another town and you were drinking."

He said it struck him so funny that he fell off the couch because he was laughing so hard. What better way to diffuse what otherwise could have become a tense situation! A great many of the events that balloon into strained, difficult situations could be turned aside in this way. As in the Hagin's case, laughter will win out over the enemy's effort.

No matter how grouchy you're feeling,

A smile is more or less healing.

It grows like a wreath

All around your front teeth

And keeps your face from congealing.

Adam Clark

8
Women's Ministries

You do not have to have a women's ministry just because you are a minister's wife. It is not obligatory! But if God leads you into it, He will have a special, unique plan for you. Ephesians 3:10 in Adam Clarke's *Commentary* speaks of the manifold wisdom of God, calling it "a wise design." Trust Him as He leads you into a wise design for women's ministry in your church.

Sometimes a women's ministry grows and grows until it is such a vital outreach, you must coordinate all the enthusiasm being generated. This is a situation that is much to be desired! When the need is obvious, it usually results in women coming forth to offer their talents.

This is where we have an opportunity to be **wise as serpents, and harmless as doves** (Matt. 10:16), because not everyone is called to be a group leader. The ones selected to lead women's ministry must be loyal, teachable, committed, faithful, and enthusiastic.

The awareness that we are asking so firmly for qualified people causes me to reflect on what God looked for when He saved us. The only quality He required was **genuine repentance and sorrow for sin.** Even after we were saved, we were instructed to simply love God and His people (1 John 5:2); study God's Word (2 Tim. 2:15); be faithful in persecution (Rev. 2:10); abhor evil and love good (Rom. 12:9); and keep His commandments. (John 14:15.)

Then why do we require so much of each other in our appointments in the church? We used to sing a chorus that said, "After all He's done for me, how can I do less than give Him my best, after all He's done for me?" That's why! We can do no less than give Him our very best in service. It is part of the New Covenant law of love. Love never settles for second best. It always wants to go the extra mile, and this is why we should be exemplary in the service we offer to Him.

We discovered quite early in our ministry that commitment, loyalty, and faithfulness do not necessarily mean a person is qualified for leadership. These are wonderful qualities, and I pray that all our churches would be full of such believers, but there has to be a gift as well.

There was a time, as pastors, that we were faced with a dilemma. We had moved from one church building that no longer met our needs into another larger building. The problem we faced was that, although there was lots of floor space, it was not suitably set up for Christian education rooms. We felt God gave us the answer, and in giving the answer, He taught us something that has been of help to us in other areas of ministry.

We left all of the children's teachers with their classes, but discovered that not all of them excelled in teaching. All of them were wonderful, dedicated, and caring people who loved each member of their class, but some did not have the ability to capture and hold their students' attention.

The solution was to appoint the capable teachers to take turns in preparing the lessons and illustrations. They would give the lesson, then each class would gather around their own teacher and discuss the material, pray together, take care of birthdays, offerings, and so forth, thereby keeping the personal touch. Certainly it was unorthodox, but more importantly, it worked! We asked our sons years later if they remembered some of them, and they were able to recall the illustrations and the lessons!

I said all of that to say this. Having a women's ministry is *not* necessary for a successful church, particularly if you do not have the right person to lead it. You may have women who excel in all of the qualities we love to see in evidence in our people, but they lack the qualities that will make them leaders whom the women will want to follow. (There is only one way you can tell if you are a leader — look behind to see if anyone is following!)

However, if you believe the time is right and there is a woman who has all the necessary qualities for leadership, go for it! Nothing will make a greater addition to a church than a women's ministry. It will touch your city through its many outreaches.

Recently we were in a growing, active church in New Orleans where one of the branches of its women's ministry is called the Rahab Ministry. Courageous women of this group go down to the French Quarter at night and witness to prostitutes, many of whom are very young girls who have run away from home. These women have had to overcome their fears, but it has become a fruitful part of that ministry. The only limits to the ways we can serve are the limits we put on ourselves!

One of the most successful ministries for women I have known was started by a friend, Barbara Cook. Jerry and Barbara pastored a very successful, growing church in the Portland, Oregon, area. When the timing was right, the women's ministry was started with a limited number of home Bible study groups. Women given to hospitality opened their homes for the groups, and those qualified to teach were appointed.

Barbara did not allow the teachers to choose the topics, but furnished a curriculum for them. There were also a few rules which applied to all groups. The women were not to talk about subjects such as children, weight, people, and so forth. The entire focus of the study was the Bible.

The studies grew so rapidly they had to keep dividing into more and more home groups. After awhile it became so unwieldy that Barbara and her board (carefully chosen) met to decide how to handle the growing attendance. Eventually, they ended up using a college auditorium in the area to handle the hundreds of women, and they met only once a month. It brought great numbers of people into the church, including many men who came because they were curious to see the cause of the positive changes in their wives!

Many wonderful auxiliary ministries were started, using women's ministry as a springboard. One very special ministry that Barbara's women's ministry gave rise to was a popular radio program called, "Touch of Beauty," carried by a Portland radio station.

There is no limit to the great service women can provide if they are given the chance. We have those who are talented with needle and thread, such as Dorcas (Acts 9:36,39); those who will minister both materially and spiritually to the needs of the body of Christ, such as Mary and Martha (Luke 10:38-40); those who will give sacrificially, like the woman with the alabaster jar (Matt. 26:7-13); and those who were at the cross (Matt. 27:56) and the first to arrive at the tomb (Matt. 28:1)!

With that supply of faithfulness and ability, when the time is right and you have counseled with your husband and prayed about it, you are ready to begin what can be one of the best things to ever happen in your church!

9
Huldah

There is a great difference between a woman "for" God and a woman "of" God. We talk to women every day who are "for" God, but the ones who are "of" God are uncommon!

A scenario to illustrate this comes from Acts 6, soon after the day of Pentecost, when the work of the Lord was going forth in great power. Mighty miracles were taking place. The dead were raised, the lame were healed, the apostles were delivered from prison, and sin was judged by sudden death. Yet in the midst of this great season of the display of God's power, we hear a strident sound — the sound of wrangling and accusation! It is the sound of discontent among women! Inconceivable!

The Grecian widows must have been complaining among themselves, feeling they were not being treated as well as the Hebrew widows. There was an uprising, significant enough to cause a meeting of the twelve disciples to take care of the problem. This happened in the Christian community of that day, and it helps to illustrate what the difference is between a woman "of" God and a woman "for" God.

When we use the word *of*, we are suggesting that the article came from the same genesis. It is not artificially produced or feigned. In other words, a woman "of" God will never be separated from the flow of God's power and ability in her life. Her life comes from within.

A woman *for* God can have all of the same desires and intents to live a consistent Christian life, but because there is no inward reserve or supply, she has to depend upon her own strength and will to live for God. Very often, because there is not an inner supply of the Spirit, her life shows a woeful lack of God's presence.

There are many examples of women "of" God mentioned in the Bible, among them Hannah, Ruth, Abigail, Esther, and Mary, the crowning example of all. Some of the greatest examples in the Bible of women "of" God are only briefly mentioned, but their lives had a telling effect.

Second Kings 22 contains the story of one of these women, Huldah. *Huldah* means "weasel," but her courage belied that meaning! The account takes place during the godly reign of Josiah, while the temple was being rebuilt. During the repair work, the book of the law was discovered, and Shaphan the scribe read it to Josiah. Josiah became very distressed because Israel had gotten so far away from the commandments written therein.

Josiah told Hilkiah the priest, Ahikam, Achbor, Asahiah and Shaphan the scribe to inquire of the Lord concerning all the things written in the book. Verse 14 indicates that instead of seeking the Lord themselves, these notable men went directly to Huldah the prophetess for assistance.

What is most remarkable about this account is described by Adam Clarke's *Commentary*: "At this time Jeremiah was certainly a prophet in Israel, but it is likely that he now dwelt at Anathoth, and could not be readily consulted; Zephaniah also prophesied under this reign, but probably he had not yet begun; Hilkiah was high priest and the priest's lips should retain knowledge. Shaphan was a scribe and must have been conversant in sacred affairs to have been at all fit for his office; and yet Huldah, a prophetess of whom we know nothing about except by this circumstance, is consulted on the meaning of the book of the law."[5]

In this short story, we can see that God often works in unexpected ways. He knows the heart of each one of us.

He knew that Huldah was the only one who would prophesy the truth about the destruction of Jerusalem. She spoke scathing words of rebuke and foretold the devastation of Jerusalem, but she spoke words of deliverance to Josiah because his heart was repentant and he feared the Lord. (v. 19.)

One of the most remarkable things about Huldah was that she was just an ordinary woman. Her husband was a tailor (v. 14) but God, Who knows our hearts, knew she would boldly and fearlessly deliver His judgment. Her name may have meant "weasel," but "lion" would have been more appropriate!

What can we learn from this personally? The primary thing we should be concerned with is the presence of God in our lives. He is revealed to others through us — how we live, how we make decisions, how we do business, and so forth. Is God big enough in our lives that He is revealed through us? He wants us to do far more than just "get along" in our daily living; He want us to be His witnesses in the earth.

Huldah, as far as everyone knew, was simply the wife of a tailor. But Hilkiah and his friends knew from the way she lived her life that God was with her and that she would prophesy the truth. That's why they sought her out. Every Christian woman who expects the move of God and cultivates His presence in her life through prayer and study will have this experience.

When we lived in Oregon in the 1970s, we had a friend who was a real prayer warrior. She was a woman of faith, and when she prayed she expected to see the answer! She tells of waking up one morning and looking out her kitchen window. Her car, which was usually parked in the driveway, was missing!

At first she was not too troubled, thinking perhaps her husband had taken it. She called him and found out that he had not, so the answer was obvious. Someone else had taken it! What she *did not do* is important. She didn't scream, she didn't cry, she didn't get mad, and she didn't call all the neighbors and spread the word. She called a prayer partner who could agree with her according to Matthew 18:19. They agreed, according to this promise, that whoever took the car would bring it back within three days.

Two days passed and nothing happened. The third day the phone rang and a young man's voice said, "Do you own a car?" He described the one he had taken. She said, "Yes, but someone has stolen it." He confessed that he was the thief and said, "I have never had so much trouble in all my life. I knew I couldn't get rid of it the way it was so I tried to disassemble it and nothing went right. All I've had is trouble. Will you come and get your car?" She said, "You stole it, you bring it back." He did, and she invited him in for coffee. Instead of calling the police, she led him to the Lord! She was truly a woman "of" God!

Prominence and renown are often as fleeting and short-lived as life itself. Many women of God such as Huldah may never be famous, but their deeds are recorded in Heaven. In Huldah's case, very few Christians are aware of her, but when the word of the Lord was needed, she was the one who was sought out!

> **For the eyes of the Lord run to and fro throughout the whole earth, to show himself strong in the behalf of them whose heart is perfect toward him.**
>
> **2 Chronicles 16:9a**

10
Selflessness

Let's face it — we live in a world where the philosophy is humanistic "me-ism"! The attitude often expressed is, "What about me?" or "What's in it for me?" One time when our daughter was little, she did not recite the scripture verse she had memorized for Sunday school. When we asked her why, she surprised us by saying, "All I'd get is a balloon!"

The materialistic attitude we sometimes have as daughters of Eve is part of our old nature that must be brought under control! It started with Satan long before the Garden of Eden, and still is a strong element to be dealt with.

Materialism is a worldly spirit, and it takes a dedicated effort to stay free of it. In Romans 12:2 AMP the writer says:

> Do not be conformed to this world (this age), [fashioned after and adapted to its external, superficial customs], but be transformed (changed) by the [entire] renewal of your mind [by its new ideals and its new attitude], so that you may prove [for yourselves] what is the good and acceptable and perfect will of God, even the thing which is good and acceptable and perfect [in His sight for you].

Another attitude of "me-ism" that we must overcome is being the center of attention. John the Baptist showed us the perfect example. He had been preaching to multitudes when Jesus came on the scene. John's disciples said that Jesus was *baptizing* and ALL men come to him (John 3:26).

Without hesitation, John said, **He must increase, but I must decrease** (John 3:30).

Say this out loud: "The ministry of the Word is the important thing, not my pride and vanity or being noticed and acclaimed." This is a very noble statement, but you have to deal with real life and emotions!

Sometimes you attend ministers' meetings and cannot join in with the glowing success reports that others are sharing. You go home feeling unfulfilled and disillusioned. This is a crossroads where you decide whether you are the focus of your life or God is.

You will either "give in" to self-pity and depression or begin to praise God for all of the good and precious aspects of your life — your faith, a husband who loves you, a beautiful family, a congregation (no matter the size) who loves you, and so forth. You have a choice. You can be the great wife of a man, or the wife of a great man!

A story is told about the great theologian Charles Spurgeon. He was walking along with a young minister who was bemoaning the fact that his congregation was small and not growing. Mr. Spurgeon asked him how many he had in his congregation and the young man answered, "About a hundred." Mr. Spurgeon replied, "Young man, that is more than you want to give God an account for." Our accountability to God grows with the addition of every precious soul that is added to our flock.

The Apostle Paul wrote to the Philippians and exhorted them to think on whatever things are true, noble, just, pure, lovely, and of good report...**if there is any virtue and if there is anything praiseworthy — meditate on these things** (Phil. 4:8, NKJV).

Very often we have to face up to unexpected emotions early on in ministry. It is easy to build a concept of the ministry in an illusory and almost fanciful image. We read books and magazines that carry biographies and stories of great men and women of God and their exploits, and we are lifted to great heights and expectations.

But these great men and women had to begin their ministry humbly, just as we do. They did not reach the pinnacle of "success," which is being an effective Christian voice with great influence, overnight. Their measure of achievement came as a result of many years of commitment and study of God's Word — not without disappointments and sometimes failures.

It was a privilege for my husband and me to sit under the ministry of Aimee Semple McPherson. She performed our wedding ceremony and dedicated our first child. Most public memory of her is founded on what was published in newspapers during her lifetime and was not flattering or accurate. She was mightily used of God and a great worldwide ministry continues to this day as a result of her dedicated life. She attained what would be considered "success" by ministering to millions and building beautiful Angelus Temple, which still stands today in Los Angeles, California.

But a great achievement like this was only realized after great trial and testing. The very first year of her ministry with Robert Semple, her first husband, ended in his death from malaria in Hong Kong. Her early years of tent evangelism in America were spent doing grueling hard work with very little help or money.

Therefore, be realistic in your expectations of a life of ministry. The promise of Jesus in Mark 10:29,30 NKJV is a great one, but read *all* of it:

> Assuredly, I say to you, there is no one who has left house or brothers or sisters or father or mother or wife or children or lands, for My sake and the gospel's,
> Who shall not receive a hundredfold now in this time — houses and brothers and sisters and mothers

and children and lands, *with persecutions* — and in the age to come, eternal life.

We cannot allow ourselves to be deceived into becoming discouraged. It is Satan's primary objective to cause God's people to fall away from the faith through persecutions and discouragement. When Jesus **appeared to put away sin by the sacrifice of himself** (Heb. 9:26b) He, once and for all, defeated Satan. When we can fully comprehend and grasp this, we will fully understand that we have victory *now,* not in the future, over sin and sickness.

When we use the Word of God as a weapon against him, Satan cannot resist or withstand the power of the Scriptures.

> **Put on God's whole armor [the armor of a heavy-armed soldier which God supplies] that you may be able successfully to stand up against [all] the strategies and the deceits of the devil.**
> **Ephesians 6:11 AMP**

Dr. Lester Sumrall, now in his eighties and continuing on in ministry with great energy and zeal, answered in three words a question asked of him by a young man. It is the answer we should all desire to give when we are in our eighties! The young man said, "Dr. Sumrall, how can you account for your many years of successful ministry?" His answer, *"I didn't quit!"*

Thank God every day for counting you faithful, putting you into the ministry (whatever your capacity) and learning to be content with such things as you have. Don't desire or covet the success of others, but only the success of what God has called you to do. Above all, live so that others will want to imitate your life!

11
The Little Member

How many times have you finished a statement and immediately said, "Oh, I wish I hadn't said that"? Do you remember cruel things that other children said to you when you were a child? Sometimes people go through life with personality defects because of some demeaning, heartless remarks that have stayed in their memory and slowly destroyed their self-image.

Proverbs 18:8 tells us, **The words of a talebearer are as wounds, and they go down into the innermost parts of the belly.** Many psychological problems of later life spring from instances when, as a child or young person, someone spoke cruelly or harshly and it cut deeply enough to lodge in the subconscious, resulting in personality flaws and insecurity.

We must cultivate a bridge from our spiritual intelligence to our tongues. Most of the responses that get us into trouble or that we are sorry for are "non-thinking" responses. We talk and talk and never think about what we are saying.

An old country farmer described someone who talked too much as having a "tongue that was tied in the middle so it could flap at both ends!" No one else could ever get into the conversation with this person.

We are the only creatures to whom God gave the ability to speak. All other creatures may communicate in some form, but they cannot speak to each other as we do. Because of this ability to communicate, God has cautioned us about the wrong use of this great gift in numerous places in the Bible. Our words can cause blessing or cursing.

Communication certainly must take place between the minister and his wife. This is important to the spiritual health of both the congregation and the home. If exchange of thoughts and ideas do not take place on a daily basis, it is like trying to accomplish a work without the left hand knowing what the right hand is doing — leading to confusion and frustration.

A researcher strapped a portable recorder and a microphone to a husband and his wife. Of the 10,080 minutes in a week, they conversed a total of 17 minutes, scarcely enough for the survival of a happy marriage! It takes some dedication to make sure there is a time for sharing goals, thoughts, and ideas, making sure we are on the same wavelength.

In Proverbs 10:19 we read, **In the multitude of words there wanteth not sin.** Ecclesiastes 5:2 says, **Be not rash with thy mouth, and let not thine heart be hasty to utter any thing before God: for God is in heaven, and thou upon earth: therefore let thy words be few.** Psalm 19:14 says, **Let the words of my mouth, and the meditation of my heart, be acceptable in thy sight, O Lord, my strength, and my redeemer.**

Recently I heard our daughter say to her eight-year-old son, Scott, after he had offered an excuse for his behavior, "This is unacceptable, Scott." Is it possible that God says the same thing to us in answer to some of the things we say in His presence?

According to James 3:2, it is a perfect person who is able to control the tongue. Verse 8 says that no one can tame it. Adam Clarke's *Commentary* states, "Nothing but the grace of God, excision, or death can bring it under submission."

"Rabbi Simeon, the son of Gamaliel, said to his servant Tobias, 'Go and bring me some good food from the market.' The servant went, and he bought tongues. At another time he said to the same servant, 'Go and buy me some bad food from the market.' The servant went and bought tongues. The master said, 'What is the reason that when I ordered thee to buy me good and bad food, thou didst bring me tongues?' The servant answered, 'From the tongue both good and evil come to man; if it be good, there is nothing better; if bad, there is nothing worse.'"[6]

The greatest miracle any of us will ever receive comes through the right use of our tongue! In Romans 10:9, we read that if we confess with our mouth the Lord Jesus and believe in our hearts that God raised Him from the dead, we shall be saved. You can scarcely find anyone who says he doesn't believe there is a God. Almost everyone believes that God exists, but those who believe in Him cannot be saved until they confess Him as Lord — with their tongue!

The practicality of disciplining the tongue shows up in experience every day. We have all reaped the rewards of both the correct and incorrect use of our tongue! As women in ministry, it is important that we seek balance in this vital area. If we talk redundantly and excessively, what we feel is worthy of saying will not be received as readily as it would if we carefully consider our words.

She opens her mouth in skillful and godly Wisdom, and on her tongue is the law of kindness [giving counsel and instruction] (Prov. 31:26 AMP). We would all do well to print this on a small card and place it where we spend a lot of time. We can memorize it, but I have memorized many good and profitable scriptures and maxims that I never think to say — until I see them!

We need to see them in order to jog our memory. If we see it and say it enough, it will become a vital part of the expression of our lives. Then, when we open our mouths, we will speak godly wisdom and kindness in our counsel and instruction.

Thank You, Lord Jesus, for seeing the desire of our hearts. We truly want to be women of God who speak according to Your Word!

12
Keeping Physically Fit

Does this subject have a place in a book written for minister's wives and women in ministry? Definitely!

I can already hear the reaction of the young housewife with several small children and all of the attendant activities that go with it! "Me, need exercise? No way!" And I understand that, having been a young mother myself.

Certainly the need for a regimen of exercise is not as crucial for young mothers as it is for women who are getting older. But we need to honestly recognize that keeping our bodies fit is much easier than letting exercise and diet go until we are faced with a major readjustment!

Webster's Dictionary defines the word *exercise* as "habitual, systematic practice, a regular series of movements designed to strengthen some part of the body or faculty." Exercise can be divided into three segments — spiritual, physical, and mental. In this chapter, I want to talk about physical exercise.

The Bible has little to say about exercise per se. Everything that was done in Bible times was done by physical labor, and the day in which they lived assured that each person would have maximum exercise from the rigors of daily living. Can you imagine the children of Israel needing an exercise program? They were physically fit enough to march around Jericho thirteen times and still have the strength to shout! (Josh. 6.) But the twentieth century is not to be compared with an era of rigorous living. We need exercise!

The human body is such a marvelous example of God's infinite wisdom. The Psalmist David said, **I will praise thee; for I am fearfully and wonderfully made: marvelous are thy works; and that my soul knoweth right well** (Ps. 139:14). He goes on to say, **When I was made in secret, and curiously wrought in the lowest parts of the earth** (v. 15).

This passage of Scripture describes the amazing and intricately careful weaving of veins, arteries, fibers, and membranes throughout the body when we are conceived in our mother's womb. The formation of the human body is also compared to the excellence of the needlework that was required of artisans who served in the furbishing of the sanctuary.

David continues, **And in thy book all my members were written** (v. 16). Adam Clarke's *Commentary* explains this. "All those members lay open before God's eyes; they were discerned by Him as clearly as if the plan of them had been drawn in a book, even to the least figuration of the body of the child in the womb."[7] We were marvelously created!

God has a plan for our spiritual life, but He also has a plan for our physical life. If we short-circuit our physical lives through lack of care, then of necessity we short-circuit what God desires for our spiritual lives. His desire for our spiritual lives and our physical being is spelled out in 3 John 2 AMP:

> Beloved, I pray that you may prosper in every way and [that your body] may keep well, even as [I know] your soul keeps well and prospers.

It is God's will that we be in health. If you have a physical body that has all its faculties, be very grateful for it. Millions of people in the world would give everything they have for a whole, healthy body, and our hearts go out to them. In view of this, how thankful we should be for what we have!

First Timothy 4:8a says, **For bodily exercise profiteth little,** and the verse goes on to say that godliness is better because it has promise for the life that now is and also the one to come. We are talking about *the life that now is;* it is in the here and now that physical exercise has a place, because those who give attention to the care of their physical bodies will be able to serve God in a much greater capacity than those who do not!

There is a plethora of devices on the market that are designed to keep us fit. Weights, bicycles, steppers, trampolines, barbells, stretchers, plus aerobics and jogging, and so forth. We have all tried one or more of them.

I remember being with a friend in a large department store that advertised all kinds of exercise equipment. My husband and I were in the market for an exercycle, so we were looking at all the different models. I climbed up on one of them for a "trial spin" and was going along quite well when, suddenly, the handlebars fell off! It caught me by surprise and I fell forward, got caught on the forward part of the frame, and couldn't get free! My friend was no help. She was folded up with laughter! Finally, I extricated myself, but that was the last exercise equipment I tried that night!

The truth is that all of these devices — much like the diets we try — are to no avail without the ingredient of "discipline." "Wishing" you were able to do more physically will not get the job done. Maybe you can wish for, long for, and crave something long enough that you will finally *do* it!

The Apostle Paul said of the contentious Corinthians, **And this also we pray, that you may be made complete** (2 Cor. 13:9 NKJV). He lived in hope that this would come to pass, but the difference between Paul's praying and our wishing is that he could not do anything about the contentious Christians. It was up to *their will.* But we can do something about ours!

At some point, our "wishing" will have to turn into "determination," and when this happens, we are on our way to becoming physically fit. *The method of exercise we use is not as important as the regularity with which we do it.*

Doing anything with consistency is our greatest battle in this arena. It is the same as when we determine we are going to read three chapters in the Bible every day. We do well for the first several days, then we miss a day. So the next day we read six chapters and do well for awhile. Then we miss two days and have to read nine chapters the next day. We don't have time, so we read six and hold over three. After that, if we miss a day or two, it gets so complicated we give up!

To begin, it is best to establish a routine of exercise that is workable and not too exhausting. As your body tones up and your breathing improves, you will begin to feel good about yourself. This will have a great effect on your productivity.

Exercising your physical body for its own good is really a spiritual activity. Your body usually takes its orders from an unsaved brain and will never offer to work that hard! All it wants to do is eat, sleep, and play.

In my husband's book, *Healing Your Insecurities*, he describes the "mind of Christ" versus the "mind of the flesh" or the "unsaved brain." It is this unsaved brain from which springs all of the carnal appetites and memories that will go into the grave and decay with the rest of the physical body when we die. It will not follow us into Heaven.

It is the same unsaved brain that will fight you every step of the way when it comes to activities that will encourage your spirit and well-being, but **we have the mind of Christ** (1 Cor. 2:16).

Don't wait for the new year! Make up your mind (the mind of Christ) that you want to be the best you can be spiritually, physically, and mentally, and put Satan on the defensive in your life. Do it *now*!

13
A Story of Submission

The Bible tells us in Ephesians 5:22, **Wives, submit yourselves unto your own husbands, as unto the Lord.** The topic of *submission* came under heavy attack in the seventies, because it was so abused and out of balance. It was so bad, there was a negative reaction from Christian women at the very mention of the word!

Submission is brought into beautiful balance in a marriage relationship if it is coupled with Ephesians 5:25: **Husbands, love your wives, even as Christ also loved the church, and gave himself for it.** What wife would not want to submit to a man who loved her with such self-sacrificing devotion? But what if the husband does not love his wife as Christ loves the Church? In fact, what if her husband isn't even saved?

We can find some answers to these questions in a most significant story about a woman of God in the book of First Samuel. It is a story that has some principles which can be of help to a woman who is entangled in a marriage where there is no longer any agreement, particularly where the husband does not (or no longer) serves God.

There are two scenarios that can be played out with this story. Both have to do with the actions and reactions of the wife who is faced with a crisis and desires to be in submission to her husband.

When a Christian wife is married to an unbeliever, God's Word does not give her the liberty of leaving him if he "is pleased to dwell with her." (1 Cor. 7:13.) This means he does not object to her going to church and serving the Lord as long as her duties as a wife and homemaker are faithfully accomplished.

The other scenario, and by far the most difficult one to bear, is the wife who is married to a man who is the "flip" side of a kind and patient man. He is cruel, impatient, and ridicules her faith. He demands things of her that are offensive to her as a Christian. It is not too often that a woman is strong, patient, and spiritually resolute enough to stay married to that man!

As always, the best way to determine how to deal with our problems is to turn to the Word of God. First Samuel 25 gives the account of Abigail and Nabal. Abigail was not only beautiful, but she was a woman of understanding and wisdom. She had to be in order to live with Nabal! She lived a life of exemplary submission until Nabal, with his evil tongue, provoked a death threat for his house and all his servants. His was the action of a man whose mind was deranged, one who did not think clearly. His name meant "fool," and so he was!

How could such a wise and beautiful woman end up married to a fool? She was probably given in marriage by her father. Today a woman can be married to a bully and wife abuser, but for different reasons. She may have married too young and didn't understand character enough to know he didn't have any! Or perhaps it was out of insecurity, the desire to get away from an unpleasant home situation, or his promise of a life of luxury that persuaded her against her own good judgment.

How much better if she had inquired of the Lord, Who knows the hearts and the future actions of all men! If we will only allow Him, He will always help us make a decision that will be best, not only for now but also for the future.

In this story David, during the period in his life when he was being pursued by Saul, had sent some of his men to ask for food from wealthy Nabal, who angrily refused to give them anything. When they returned and told David of Nabal's words, his reaction was swift. They mounted their horses and were on their way to annihilate Nabal and all his house!

In the meantime, one of the servants ran to Abigail and told her what was happening. Immediately she ordered servants to prepare food, then she set out to meet David, who was even then on his way to destroy them all. She met him on his way to her house and said, "Let this iniquity be upon me. Nabal, though he is a fool, is still my husband, but if I had seen the young men first, the answer would have been different and you would not have come here to shed blood without cause" (paraphrased). Her great act of courage and wisdom stopped David in his rash act. He repented of his vengeful intentions and told her to go back to her home in peace.

Justice was ultimately meted out to everyone concerned. Ten days later Nabal was dead. Abigail became the beloved wife of David, who had proved his stature by listening to the wisdom of one who was less than he. His oath to kill was bad, but it would have been much worse if he had followed through.

When you first read this account, you may think Abigail was an unsubmitted wife, but she must have had many opportunities to prove her submission. If one lives with a "fool," the life of submission will be filled with challenges!

There are times in this life when a Christian woman who is living with an unsaved mate is asked (or ordered) to do something contrary to her Christian faith. If that husband, though unsaved, is a reasonable man, she can reason with him and decline his request.

However, if a woman is married to an angry man who is subject to irrational demands or to one who is addicted to alcohol or other mind-altering drugs, and he requires things of her that are in direct contradiction to the Bible, she could, with a right spirit and wisdom, look for an alternative to his demand.

I remember listening to a woman who was married to a man addicted to alcohol. When he was sober, he was a wonderful and kind man. When he drank, he became angry and unreasonable — completely different than when he was sober. When he drank and demanded that his Christian wife drink or go to the bar with him, she refused kindly, knowing in her heart, "I am not being unsubmitted. If my husband was sober and in his right mind, he would not ask me to do this. I am submitted to my husband when he is in his right mind."

This path is not for one who is faint-hearted. Only a woman whose relationship with the Lord is very real could endure and survive this extreme test of faith and courage. Whatever decisions a Christian woman makes in a difficult situation, such as any of those discussed in this chapter, if that decision is based upon a close and secure relationship with the Lord Jesus, He will walk with her, giving her wisdom and strength for every challenge.

14
Dealing With Mistakes, Mischief, and Malice

Some may think the title of this chapter contradicts the positive gospel message we teach. However, to recognize a spiritual enemy who is dedicated to the destruction of the Church does not contradict the gospel. In fact, overcoming the enemy is a significant part of the gospel and is considerable good news! When we comprehend his devious power to destroy and ruin lives, we can avoid becoming his victims.

One evening after my husband had preached a message from his book entitled, *Ready Or Not . . . Here Comes Trouble*, a young couple came up to him and said, "We don't need the book. We'll never have troubles." My husband handed them the book anyway and said, "Take it, it's free." The content of the message was that, by simply living in a devil's world, Christians will face many trials and temptations, but they have power over the enemy in the name of Jesus.

If there is anyone anywhere who thinks they can live a life immune from trouble and temptation, they have claimed a lifestyle to which even the Lord Jesus did not attain. **For we have not an high priest which cannot be touched with the feeling of our infirmities, but was in all points tempted as we are, yet without sin (Heb. 4:15).**

The title of this chapter does sound negative, but negatives are never neutralized by being ignored! They must be challenged and corrected. To be honest, none of us are involved in ministry very long before we become aware that we must be prepared to handle disagreeable situations. If we do not handle them, they will destroy our ministry and all God wants to do.

Within the local church, if the congregation is walking in the light of the Word of God, you will find peace and goodwill. But there are times when that peace is disturbed by the enemy, who works through weak or immature Christians in gossip, jealousy, accusation, backbiting, etc. At this point we must be spiritually and emotionally prepared to deal with the situation.

Avoiding and putting an end to adversity among the brethren is part of the fight of faith! Satan is a defeated foe, but he has access to the body of Christ wherever there is a weakness. He can cause great damage if we do not move in the power and wisdom available to us through the guidance of the Holy Spirit. James 1:5 tells us that if we lack wisdom, all we need to do is ask God and it will be given.

In this great ongoing adventure of ministry, there will be many opportunities and challenges that will cause us to turn to the Holy Spirit for help, comfort, and guidance. We will need to seek Him earnestly for wisdom in dealing with emotional and serious issues that often arise. Most important, we must discern whether actions on the part of others are mere mistakes, mischief, or pure malice. Satan uses any opportunity to wreak havoc among the saints.

Mistakes should be easily forgiven, because we all make them. "Forgive and forget" should be the theme of our lives concerning them. But mischief is a little different, because it usually involves some level of injury or hurt to others. The reaction of those who are the object of mischief could prove very negative and ultimately do damage to many others.

Foolish talking and jesting, like uncleanness and covetousness, should be avoided. the Bible says they **should not be once named among you, as becometh saints** (Eph. 5:3,4). This passage of Scripture goes on to mention other exercises of the flesh such as filthiness. We are strongly admonished to encourage one another instead of indulging in these sins.

As women of the Word of God, our example of doing the Word will be far more powerful than anything we could say or teach.

I have a good friend who is a pastor's wife. She is gifted with wisdom, and I value her friendship highly. The reason I mention her in this context is that the church they pastor went through a difficult time with certain individuals in the membership. My purpose is not to highlight the trouble, but to emphasize her demeanor in the midst of it.

My friend acted as a peacemaker whenever possible and kept an unfailing positive attitude. She is a woman of prayer whose obvious faith and perseverance were a great example to every woman in her church. As a result, the ladies followed her example and great turmoil was neutralized.

Because of the troubles that arise in congregations, it has been apparent that Satan has had access to many Christians in one area of their lives or another. For that reason, you must always remember to **take great care, then, how you live** (Eph. 5:15, TCNT). Adam Clarke's Commentary says of this verse, **and behave yourselves so that your enemies may never be able to say that you are holy in your doctrines and profession, but irregular in your lives.**[8] This accurately describes a wavering Christian who says one thing and does another.

Early in our ministry we were called to pastor an established church where the congregation consisted of many wonderful, dedicated Christians. However, we faced a difficult situation that had been allowed to develop over a number of years. One very strong couple had slowly gained power and control in the church by holding two of the most influential positions, head of the church board and adult Bible teacher.

As newcomers, it took us some time to assess there was a problem. There was nothing wrong with a couple holding those positions in a church, but eventually we became aware that the enemy had deceived them into believing they were indispensable and should receive favored treatment over anyone else in the church.

Fully understanding the possible negative consequences, we determined not to bow to the principle that had put them in the controlling position in the first place, which was their favored status. My husband put an end to it, and not long after they left the church.

We took authority over the enemy, and in Jesus' name we prohibited him from taking advantage of the situation to work confusion in the congregation. As the wife of the pastor, my posture and that of all women who held any position of authority in the church was strategic.

The attitude we took was based upon Ephesians 4:29: **Let no corrupt communication proceed out of your mouth, but that which is good to the use of edifying, that it may minister grace to the hearers.** Our example stopped criticism and God was able to continue working in the lives of the church members.

When circumstances like these take place in a church, it is tremendously important for everyone to take great care how they live, especially the pastor, his wife, and every staff member. Churches can come through great trials and tests and stay intact when an example of grace and maturity is set by those in leadership.

Now I beseech you, brethren, by the name of our Lord Jesus Christ, that ye all speak the same thing and that

there be no divisions among you, but that ye be perfectly joined together in the same mind and in the same judgment (1 Cor. 1:10). When a congregation practices this verse of Scripture by dealing fairly and compassionately with mistakes, avoiding and discouraging mischief, and putting away all malice, God can move mightily in their midst!

15
Competition
By Dr. Roy Hicks

When Margaret asked me to read some of her new book, I enjoyed it so much that I volunteered to write a chapter from the perspective of a husband! We have lived together as husband and wife for over fifty years, and I sometimes say, with a smile, that we have a perfect marriage! There is truth in this statement that can work for those who understand the true meaning of the Greek word for *perfect*.

Hebrews 13:21 says, **Make you *perfect* in every good work to do his will.** In this verse, the word *perfect* is the Greek word *katartizo*, which means "adjust and repair." I say jokingly, "If Margaret isn't adjusting, I'm repairing, or vice versa!" A good marriage lived daily on this basis will be a happy one! *Rather than endeavoring to find which one to blame, why not adjust or repair, or both?*

Adam and Eve would have had a much better marriage had they practiced "adjusting and repairing," but before we criticize them, we must appreciate what they faced. First of all, there was no former experience from which to learn. They had never seen each other before, let alone lived together! There were no other people to look to as an example or from whom they could receive advice.

Keep in mind that these first created beings were given a very strong will, just as we have. When God explained to Adam that they had access to all of the fruit trees except one, Eve also knew. Their challenge of the "do's" and "don'ts" was the same as it is for us today.

We call Eve the first woman shopper and Satan the first fast-talking salesman! When she was challenged, her answer showed that she knew not to eat of the tree and that death would be the penalty for disobedience. (Gen. 3:3.) At this point, a very dangerous game began, the game of *competition*.

Satan, in competition with God, knew the game well from past experience. Competition first began when he challenged God over the ownership of His throne. Even though his willful rebellion sealed his ultimate destruction, Satan came in the same rebellious spirit to draw Adam and Eve into his damnable net.

First he confronted Eve with a challenge to play the deadly game of competition, then Adam joined in. God had clearly warned them that they were not to eat of the tree of the knowledge of good and evil or else they would die, so when they chose to eat, it was with full knowledge of the consequences.

The entire world was drawn into the results of their fall. Every world government with its kings, presidents, and dictators are in power through this system of competition. The history of the Napoleons, the Hitlers, the Stalins, and the Mussolinis is evidence that the spirit of competition reigns!

Competition usually begins when one is challenged about what they know or can do: "I know more than you know." "I am stronger than you." "My daddy can whip your daddy." On and on we go! On top of that, from early childhood we hear the word "don't" more often than any other word. It is a bona fide word in child training, but it also challenges!

As we grow, we become more and more involved in competition with our parents, siblings, playmates, and school teachers. Therefore, it is only natural to see competition raise its ugly head later on when we marry. After all, many of us can remember the competition between our parents as they were raising us! However, we can use the Word to overcome this temptation.

Instead of falling in with the system and challenging your spouse just to provoke them to strife and anger, why not put your hand over your mouth to keep it quiet! Avoid responses such as: "I believe the President is doing a good job."/"I don't." "I like our new Pastor."/"He's not as good as the last one." "Let's go to the coast on our vacation."/"You always have to go to the mountains." Practice the important principle of *lay your hand upon your mouth when you have thoughts of evil* (Prov. 30:32).

Webster's Dictionary explains the word *evil* as "anything that causes harm, pain, misery, or disaster." Few things cause more harm than gossip, criticism, and disagreement only for the sake of disagreeing! Words that stir up anger and strife in a marriage relationship are especially wicked, because they tear down and destroy what a man and woman commit to when they take the marriage vows — the building of a strong and loving relationship.

In view of this problem where spouses compete with one another, it is amazing that some marriages last as long as they do. Single boy meets single girl, and as conversation begins, each revealing their philosophy of life, usually it is apparent that there is disagreement before they really know each other, each of them having come from a totally different home environment. Only those who refuse to allow a demonic spirit of competition to enter their relationship will have a good, happy marriage — which makes a solid, powerful ministry for the Lord.

Husbands and wives in ministry, in order to be successful, must conquer the insecurities that surface when a spirit of satanic competition comes against them to pit them against one another. All great ministries, including those of Aimee Semple McPherson, Smith Wigglesworth, John Wesley, Martin Luther and many others, became great because they ignored criticism, resisted the temptation to compete, and chose to walk in love instead!

Endnotes

[1] John Locke, "Of the Conduct of the Understanding," *International Thesaurus of Quotations* (Harper & Row, 1970), 1706.

[2] Adam Clarke, *Clark's Commentary*, Vol. 6 (Abingdon Cokesbury Press), 463.

[3] Henrietta Mears, *Four Hundred Thirty One Quotes From the Life of Henrietta Mears* (Gospel Light Press, 1970), 38.

[4] Linda Dillow. *Creative Counterpart* (Nelson House Publishers, 1977), 92, 93.

[5] Clarke, *Op. Cit.*, Vol. 2, p. 560.

[6] *Ibid.*, Vol. 6, p. 816.

[7] *Ibid.*, Vol. 6, p. 816.

[8] *Ibid.*, Vol. 3, p. 665.

Margaret Hicks is the wife of Dr. Roy H. Hicks, former General Supervisor of the International Foursquare Churches. She has been active in ministry with him since their graduation in 1944 from LIFE Bible College in Los Angeles.

Dr. and Mrs. Hicks have ministered as pastors in the states of Ohio, Nebraska, and New York, then as District Supervisors in Western Canada and in the Northwest United States before going to Headquarters in 1985. They have travelled widely and Margaret has been privileged to speak to many women's groups, both at home and abroad.

Mrs. Hicks is the author of one mini-book entitled, "The Christian Woman's Answer to Aging," and has assisted in the writing of many books authored by her husband. Their oldest son went home to be with the Lord in the fall of 1994, and they have another son, one daughter, and three grandchildren.